SINGING MAKES YOU HAPPY

10 Minute Workout for a Beautiful Voice

Dr. des. Christin Bonin

SINGING MAKES YOU HAPPY

10 Minute Workout for a Beautiful Voice

Dr. des. Christin Bonin

Impressum

The German National Library lists this publication in the Deutsche Nationalbibliografie; detailed bibliographic data are available on the Internet at http://dnb.dnb.de."

© 2021 Christin Bonin

Illustration: Gunter Hansen, Gerhard Schlegel

Printing and Publishing: BoD – Books on Demand, Norderstedt

ISBN: 978-3-7534-5424-5

TABLE OF CONTENTS

PREFACE

Singing makes you happy.
"Lucky those who can sing," you might say.
Everybody can sing.
Don't you believe me? Give it a try.
Singing is a blessing.
Suddenly, we have a good posture, much better breathing, and a more intense facial expression.
Singing is probably the ultimate form of expression for people without using any tools.
A beautiful voice gives a whole new dimension to words.
Of course, we admire virtuoso instrumentalists, solo dancers, and painters. But when we listen to a beautiful voice, it goes deep into our hearts, and we remember it for a very long time, more than anything else.
You look after your clothes; you train your body, and you improve your expertise.
What about your voice?
Make something out of it. Make yourself happy and experience your voice in a new way.
In the age of YouTube and iTunes, we are virtually flooded by music, but what do we take from it personally? In the 20th century, singing was much more a part of everyday life. People sang at home, at school, everywhere. Nowadays, we don't sing anymore; we walk the roads with our headphones, sending a text or an email.
"I will make a fool of myself if I take singing classes."
Do you make a fool of yourself if you take advice from a doctor?
Taking classes will help you learn the DOs and the DONTs of singing and show you what you already know.
"My voice sounds horrible. There's nothing you can do about it."

Yes, you can.
Our singing voice needs training, whereas we develop our ability to speak by imitation only.

When we learn to speak, we imitate our parents and our entire social environment, including their weaknesses and mistakes, their dialect-driven vocal colors, and more.

A healthy baby does not lose its voice by crying. The energetic power of a baby's voice is quite impressive.

Babies know how to do it right by instinct.

So, to get a beautiful voice, you only need to rediscover and draw upon your innate skills.

But how do you do it?

Practice. Only for a couple of minutes every day - or simply as often as possible.

You will hear the difference soon, and you will be amazed by the quick success!

I intend to give you some simple advice and exercises so you can experience your own voice. Therefore, I will spare you physiological insights and too many technical details.

After all, you just want to sing!
Give it a try.
You won't regret it.

Make yourself happy.

Sing!

Christin Bonin

1 INTRODUCTION

1.1 The Voice as an Instrument

Our voice serves as a role model for all musical instruments.
It is not only based on the larynx and vocal cords; it is a whole-body instrument.

Let's compare our voice to a guitar, for example.

The resonating cavities in our head and the upper part of our body form a human resonance chamber that almost resembles a guitar.

Depending on body height and weight, it might resemble more a violin – or a string bass. ☺

Take a look at a YouTube video of vocal cords, and you will realize that they fulfill the same function that strings do on a guitar: They start to resonate, and the resonating air produces a tone in the resonance chamber. The tone pitch largely depends on the tenseness of the string on the guitar. Regarding our instrument "voice," our vocal cords are responsible for singing on the correct pitch. It is achieved by voice placement and support. On a guitar, that corresponds to the bottom fixings of the string and the tuners on the guitar head.

Et voilà, here comes our voice as a musical instrument!

1.2 Breathing

If you want to sing, you need air. Sometimes you even need a lot of air.

Filling your body with air is basically like pouring water into a glass:

It means you breathe from the bottom up to fill your body or, strictly speaking, your lungs with air.
First, your belly expands, then your sides and a little bit your back, and only then your chest should rise.

Attention: Keep your shoulders down!
Unless you do, you cannot stand upright - look into the mirror and see how funny you look with your shoulders pulled up.

Now you inhaled perfectly. Easy, isn't it?
Your body is filled with air now, and just like a well-inflated air mattress, your body should be much more voluminous.

If you were "high breathing" so far, which means you inhaled only into your chest, maybe even with your belly muscles sucked in, then start to practice perfect breathing by inhaling deeply into your belly, your sides, and your upper chest.

If you find that too difficult, practice lying on your back:

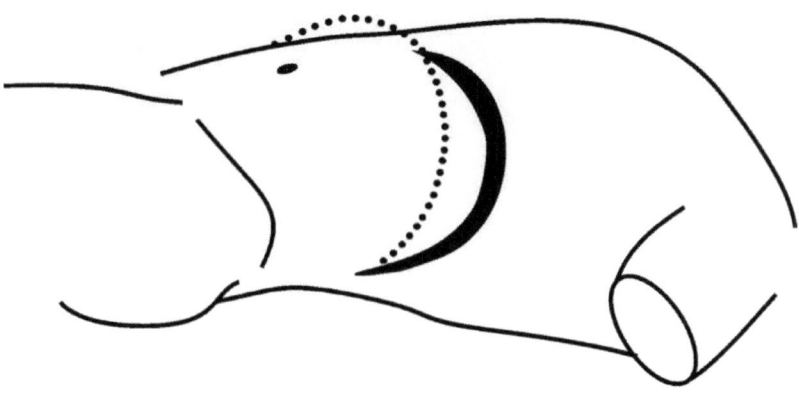

Place a book onto your belly right above your belly button and take a deep breath so that your stomach seems to expand and your chest rises slightly.

Then exhale, producing the sound "sssss," and release the energy very slowly.

The best time to practice this exercise is when you lie in bed. Experience how relaxing it is, and you will sleep like a baby.

1.3 Voice Placement

When singers speak of voice placement, they mean the intensive use of the head resonators for producing a sound.

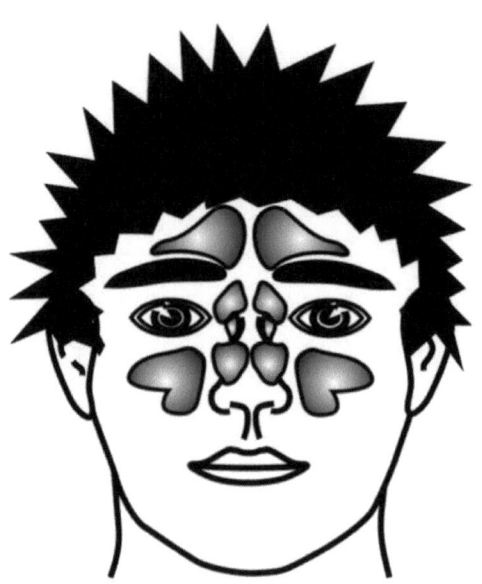

We don't think about it when we speak.
Words come out of your mouth, and that's it.

But when you sing, your voice should "ring," which means that your rather dull speaking voice needs a fuller sound. I'm not talking of loudness. I will come back to that later.

You produce sound by letting the tone resonate, or more precisely, by allowing the air resonating in your top resonators (resonating cavities) I mentioned before: your paranasal sinuses, frontal sinuses, and all other tiny holes in your head. Know that letting your voice vibrate in these headspaces only, without adding anything else, is often called singing in head voice.

Your voice sounds very cute then, clear, and very soft. However, you only use part of your voice, but this part of your voice is the gist of the matter:

Without this voice placement, you cannot sing beautifully.

Never forget that.

1.4 Support

If you want to increase the beautiful sound you achieved by practicing your voice placement, you must add an "amplifier."
The so-called voice support will increase your sound and add more volume to your voice.
What does that mean?
If you inhale properly, air fills your body and widens it.
Then, if you start speaking or singing, you usually simply release the energy until your body is "empty" and then inhale once again.
Your body loses energy just like an air mattress loses air!

That is the wrong way to do it.

So, what does "support" mean?

"Support your voice" means:
While you sing, you always try to keep your muscles tensed at the energetic level you achieved after you inhaled adequately.
That way, your instrument maintains its shape, your resonators remain active, and your voice energetic.

That's it.

2 THE 10 MINUTE WORKOUT PROGRAM

2.1 Exercise 1: Warming Up and Voice Placement Exercise

Before you start, be sure you change your voice from "speaking" to "singing."
Be it sports or singing; any good workout starts with a warming-up exercise.

Inhale as described before and then softly in a low voice, sing the Italian vowels A E I O U on the first three notes of a scale up and down again, and while you do so, put your finger to the root of your nose. Imagine your tones float away like soap bubbles.

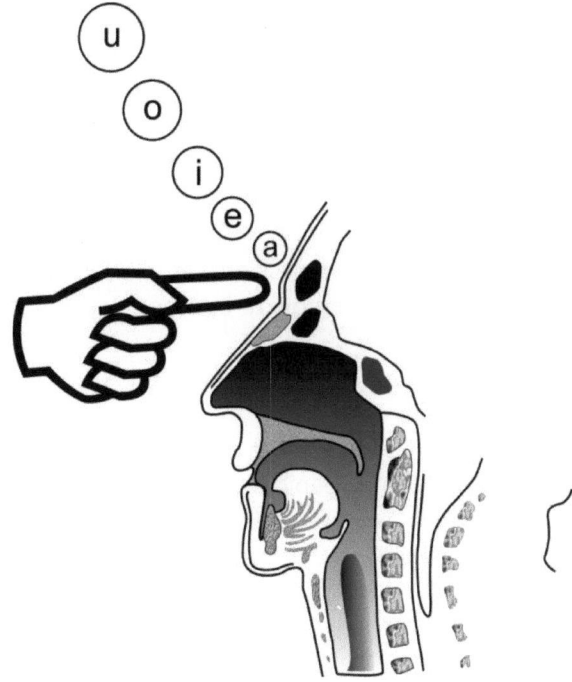

If you use too much air and too little energy, the excess air will "flood" out of your mouth. In this case, imagine using just enough air for each vowel to make the tone audible. Once you have finished, just let the excess air out, inhale again and repeat the exercise singing a half step up. Repeat the exercise several times. Only sing the scale up as far as you feel comfortable with without getting louder. Make sure your body doesn't tense and keep a relaxed but upright posture.

On the Download Track 1, "Warming Up and Voice Placement Exercise," you can listen to a demonstration, and then you can practice along afterward.

2.2 Exercise 2: Activating Your Voice Support

To activate your voice support, you must lower your diaphragm. Chances are you last felt your diaphragm when you had a side stitch. You need your abs to train your diaphragm muscle.

That doesn't mean you need a six-pack for singing, even though it might look great on you!

But if your muscles are not strong at all, you can't feel them, and therefore you can't learn how to use them.

So, here comes your abs workout for singers!

You must know that flexible abs play an essential role.
Tensing your belly and keeping it tight will lead you nowhere.
That's why in this exercise, we train your abs to become energized but remaining flexible so you can use them properly for singing.

As soon as you press the upper end of your straight abs outwards, your diaphragm lowers. With your diaphragm in a downward position, you gain support.

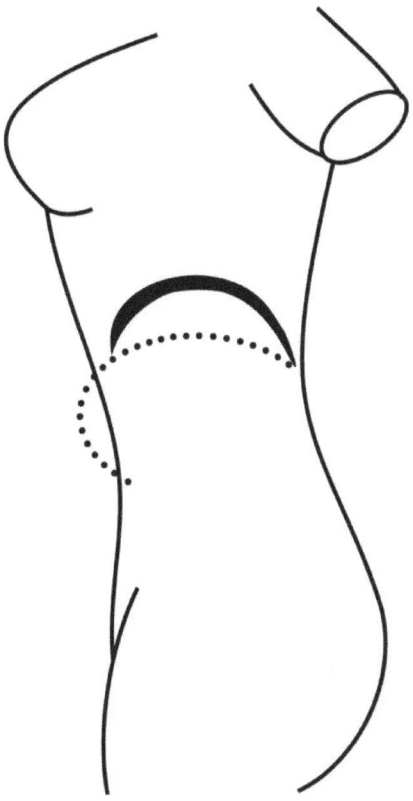

Now sing with enthusiasm the syllable "schni" (Italian vowel i) a tonic triad up and back down, pronouncing schni-i-i-i.
Make sure you give your abs a slight push on the "schni" and each of the following three "i." So on each tone, your belly extends outwards. On your fourth "I," hold your abs tense and sing a long "i" on a triad.

Place your hand right above your belly button and feel that movement.

This exercise will only work, however, if you let go between the tones. But please make sure you don't breathe after each "i." Otherwise, you breathe into a relaxed diaphragm position which causes high breathing. That happens very quickly; we often tend to high breathing in our hectic and stressful everyday life.

So, make sure you inhale as explained at the beginning of this book.

Simply imagine you play ping pong with your upper abs, and the long "i" on the triad is your smash:

Let's start singing!
On the Download Track 2, "Activating Your Voice Placement," you can hear me demonstrate it ... and then it's your turn!

2.3 Extending Your Range

2.3.1 Exercise 3: Building Up Energy

Let's start to train your range now.

It is all about building up the energy with your breathing and then actively keeping it up. In other words, you actively prevent your instrument from collapsing.

Singing exercises will warm up your voice and help you understand the typical sound structure of our occidental music and its system of scales and cadences consisting of tonic, subdominant, and dominant. In case you are interested, take a deeper look into musical theory. However, to start singing, all you need is your voice.

If you want to sing several tones between two breaths, you have to know how much air you will need right from the beginning. You also have to make yourself aware of how far the lowest and the highest tones are apart. That will keep you from getting stuck because you cannot sing further up or down all of a sudden.

Practice the following two exercises, and you will get a sense of how extensive the range is on a small vocal line:

Take an upright posture, and while you exhale, stretch your arms sideways like wings. At the end of this movement, breathe and sing the syllable "ni" on the first tone of the exercise. Now, without breaking the musical line, move your "arm wings" downwards like a spread eagle and sing the Italian vowel "A" on a quint upwards (the fifth tone of the scale), and then sing it back again to the note you sang on "ni."

I demonstrate to you how that sounds on the Download Track 3, "Building Up Energy," ... and then it's your turn again!

When you practice, make sure that the first (= lowest) tone sounds just as bright as the second (= highest) in your voice placement. Only then, your voice will sound beautiful throughout the entire exercise, and your vocal color will not change. Unfortunately, we tend to sing low tones stronger and louder. For most of us, this is relatively easy to do. But we forget that the top notes don't tolerate this dark vocal color.

Bear in mind: Modesty is beautiful! So please start singing correctly, bright and soft, before getting loud.

You should also be aware that the purpose of this exercise is how you move your arm wings downwards:

Once the eagle beats his wings, he pushes air downwards, and consequently, his body rises.

If you carry out the movement in full awareness, you automatically tense your abs, press your belly slightly outwards, and with it, you support your tone. Your tone sounds stronger and does not go flat. When singing down the scale again, you must simply keep up the energy, and here you are: Every tone sounds great, has the same vocal color, and the same loudness.
Singing with a beautiful voice is really easy!

2.3.2 Exercise 4: Increasing Energy and Managing Air

The following exercise works according to the same principle. The only difference is that you must sing the first tone even brighter and softer than the second tone because now the notes are far more apart (an octave leap).

Looking at it from a physical point of view, you nearly double the frequency between the first and the second tone, which means you double the number of vibrations per second. If you sing the first tone too loud, it takes up so much place in our top resonators that there is no place left for the higher frequency.
That's why it is so important to sing the bottom tone light and bright.

Sounds logical, doesn't it?

If you now sing from the highest tone down the scale, you must manage your air correctly so you can sing back down to the note you started.

Hopefully, you remembered filling your body with enough air when you started the exercise, just like a gigantic glass of water; otherwise, you will indeed run out of air.

Luckily, you can learn how to manage your air. That's what this exercise is all about, and it will help you with many songs.

Give it a try: On the Download Track 4, "Increasing Energy and Managing Air," I demonstrate how it works ... and then you'll try!

2.4 Extending Your Range Downwards

2.4.1 Exercise 5: Softly Awakening Your Chest Register

Having practiced the exercises correctly so far, you will certainly have developed an excellent and consistent sound by now, and you will be able to catch higher tones. You might even be able to sing higher than you used to sing before.

But there is more than just singing high tones. Sometimes you will need to sing lower than you usually do – and all of a sudden, you only produce hot air!

Therefore, this chapter will teach you how to let your voice resonate in your body, strictly speaking in your chest register.

In my first chapter, I introduced the notion of "head voice."

Now let's activate your chest voice.

What does that mean?

Again, let's compare our human resonance chamber to a guitar.

The upper part is more petite and corresponds to our head register, our top resonators.

The bottom part is more prominent and represents the chest register, our chest resonators.

Head register and chest register are also called head voice and chest voice. It's just another word for the same thing.

I prefer using the name "body sound" rather than "chest register," so you will imagine your chest voice as lovely, big, and a whole-body experience. Depending on your physique, you should not accept a weak sound just because your chest may resemble more closely a chicken breast than the chest size of a terminator!

Now, you want to increase your excellent and supported sound on low tones too. Sing the Italian syllable "ia" on a stepwise chord down the scale and actively allow your sound to get darker, but without letting the tone drop or without pressing it down.

On the contrary:
When singing down the scale, imagine that you are climbing the stairs with two shopping bags!

You should even really try that while singing!

It is a lot of fun, and you may soon find that your voice "sits" better, and you will catch each tone properly.

Because when you do that, you cannot help tensing your body, so it is almost impossible to let the tones drop or press them downwards.

Listen to the Download Track 5, "Softly Awakening Your Chest Register," and check how that sounds - and then sing along with solid and well-supported tones on your way home from your grocery shopping!

2.5 Varying the Vocal Colors

In the classical singing technique, the so-called *bel canto*, which means "beautiful singing," the aim is always to achieve a perfectly balanced sound. In modern music, the laws are different.

Modern music developed from spirituals and soul music.
Thus, in modern music, spirit and soul play a much more significant role than a perfect sound.
Here, the expression of emotions has always been more crucial.
"I'm singing with my stomach," Janis Joplin answered when people asked her where she took all the power from for her rock screams.
Singing out of your belly does not only mean getting the power from your body center. It's more than that. It refers to the emotions behind the lyrics and how music transports these to the audience.

Nevertheless, over the years, the perfection of *bel canto* has mingled with the expressive emotional power of spirituals and soul music. Vice-versa, the musical and vocal benchmarks have become just as high in modern music. So, neither a cute girly voice nor a loud screamy one will be able to win anything at a contest.

A good pop singer combines perfectly balanced tones with an expressive emotional sound.

"Sing your soul out" clearly describes best how deep-felt emotions need to be when combined with musical skill.
One or the other is not enough anymore.
Now train your newly acquired singing abilities and combine voice placement and support with the emotions you wish to express.

"In joy and in sorrow, be thoughtful;

Long and fearful in suspended pain;

Rejoicing to heaven, grieving to death;

Blessed alone is the soul that loves."

J.W. Goethe

Goethe's enthusiastic proverb clearly expresses what a song is all about! Almost every song is about love: loving somebody else, loving music, your car, your dog – loving life itself! You have to deliver changing emotions, deep doubts, big hopes, endless longing, painful loss, total desperation, final breakdown, and outdazzling blissful happiness by singing the lyrics and letting the music sound in a way that the audience can feel it.

Many people are doing the right thing by instinct, but often the dose is not correct.

Depending on the person's temper and nature, the dose is sometimes too much and sometimes too little.

Sometimes in an abundance of passion, emotions turn into the opposite, and an enthusiastic voice cracks, or a strong rock tone suddenly turns into a shriek.

You can practice and learn how to get that under control.

2.5.1 Developing Vocal Color

The following exercise will help you practice bringing the sound of your voice from a soft and light tone to a loud and intense one. You will be able to express various changes of emotions: For example, cheerful ignorance changes into mad fury and despair, like it is the case in many songs when a woman or man is abandoned or betrayed; or quiet sadness develops and finally becomes a significant moment of happiness.

Happy = quiet, light, and bright voice

Furious = loud, strong, and dark voice

Start singing up a scale with a very light, bright tone, and on the 6th tone, add your support ("eagle wings").

Unlike in "real life," a singer may not shout or yell for happiness nor despair. If your voice sounds "shouty," chances are you started too loud, or with too "thick" a tone, you lost your voice placement on the way, or you didn't inhale enough air.

Listen carefully to how the first five tones must sound, so the higher tones sound strong and beautiful:

In Download Track 6, "Developing Vocal Color," we start with a soft and quiet voice before the tones become more and more energetic.

2.5.2 Changing Sound

We often hear a voice that begins with a lot of energy in the low tones and becomes so elegant, bright, and light in the high tones.

You can do that as well.

The trick to make it work is to avoid singing with the same energy from low to high as long as you can but changing to a lighter and brighter sound at the right time.

You need to practice finding out how far up you can sing with energy and at what point you must change to a brighter and lighter tone to finish the scale. Here, each voice is different. From experience, it's mostly the change from E to F or from B to C that makes the so-called passaggio difficult. Therefore, it is advisable for most people to already sing the tones before a little brighter and not use too much air. Sometimes it's the change from A to B flat or from E flat to E. Each voice has a unique timbre or vocal color, and the singer needs to find out how it works at its best by practicing.

Isn't it amazing that the notes E and F and B and C are just those keys with no black keys between them on a piano keyboard? Indeed, this is not by accident. This change of vocal registers is precisely one of the most crucial aspects of vocal technique.

Nevertheless, don't forget to express your emotions:
Imagine, for example, you start singing in a rage, and then your anger cools down. Or you start singing in sheer happiness, and then you become more melancholy and more thoughtful or even sad.
Try that. It works!

Full of joy, excited

Melancholic, thoughtful, sad

In Download Track 7, "Changing Sound," we start with an energetic sound and then softly change to a quiet and light sound.

2.5.3 Sound Variations

The most exciting aspect of modern music is sound variation within the same song when a voice starts energetic, becomes very soft, and ends up in a bright sound.
Again, emotions can help you find the right power of expression:
You start "grumpy," which means you are a bit angry; then you think about it, you calm down; and finally, when you regard the whole thing positively, you feel happy and released.

Angry, grumpy

Thoughtful, more relaxed

Full of joy, excited

Download Track 8 "Sound variations" demonstrates how it sounds when you start more energetic, then sing a quieter passage, and finally end up loud again in the high tones.

When you practice this, you must pay attention to both transitions:

When you change from energetic to light, you must find the right moment to perform the "thicker" tone a little brighter. After that, when you wish to sing with a little more energy on higher notes, make sure not to start with too much power too early; otherwise, you may run out of air.

Managing air is extremely important: When you start singing with too much energy or sing too quietly in the higher passage (your transition between high and low, also called *passaggio*), you will run out of air in high tones.
It's not a healthy choice for your voice either: As soon as you run out of air - by instinct - you tense your muscles to compensate. In doing so, you needlessly subject your voice muscles to fatigue. Balancing the voice between energetic/loud and soft/quiet is a singer's task of a lifetime.

Any singer can master the art of balancing energy by training. "All the time energetic" is just as boring as "all the time soft." Each time you sing, enjoy discovering your self-created tone mixture and make it sound better!

3 SINGING

If you want to learn how to sing, the most important thing of all is:

Sing!
As often as you can.
As much as you want.
For as long as you like.

Don't let anyone else intimidate you. Whoever sticks up the nose or makes snide remarks - is simply jealous!

You need the courage to sing - and this is where sometimes even immense talents fail.

Singing is not just about the correct pitch. With every song we sing, we deliver an attitude towards life and present longing, happiness, or hurt.
Very often, we automatically choose songs that match our present mood, and that's why we feel "caught." After all, you don't want anyone else to know that when you listen to "I will always love you," you think of the love you lost, or whatsoever you feel when you hear "I can't get no satisfaction."

That's why we hesitate to sing about what moves our soul because we don't want to reveal too much of ourselves.

But don't worry: It's just how YOU feel about it!

Nobody in the audience thinks about whether you sing the song from a personal perspective or whether you simply want to perform a great piece of music to them.

All the audience wants is good entertainment, and if you sing beautifully, you deliver just that!

You sing beautifully when you brilliantly find the right pitch, easily without trying too hard, when you keep the rhythm and deliver the feeling of enjoying yourself!

If you love to sing, the tips in this book will help you make good progress.

On top – if you want to go further, you will need the help of a voice teacher. And don't believe the old wives' tale that some professional singers have taught themselves how to sing without a voice teacher! They always are "coached," which is the same but sounds cooler ...
Without a teacher, advisor, coach, someone to give you feedback, it is hard to learn anything.
Boris Becker did not teach himself how to play tennis, and Luciano Pavarotti undoubtedly would not have become a world-famous singer without a voice teacher.
In fact, "talent" is just a part of success in the art business:
Courage, effort, perseverance, and endless love for what you wish to achieve, are much more important than the so-called "Super Talent."

Sing.

Learn new songs and enjoy increasing your repertoire of songs you practiced and learned properly.

You have no idea of what to sing?
Let me suggest a couple of songs you might enjoy singing:

Download Track 9: La-la-la
Download Track 10: Street of Dreams
Download Track 11: Christmas under Palm Trees

4 LOVE AND PASSION

As I made clear in the previous chapter, the emotional aspect of singing is essential. So let me add some words to it.

"Singing makes you happy," that's a scientific fact.
"Singing is healthy." That is another fact.

Still, some people are afraid of it.
What exactly do those people fear?
In most cases, the answer is: "Making a fool of themselves."
That's human nature: we would rather miss something that will do us good than taking the risk of being laughed at.
Hmm, laughed at – by whom? The people who love you?
Indeed, if you participate in a television singing contest, know that you take the risk of having to listen to silly comments on your voice. If you expose yourself to that, you should be aware that it is just an entertainment show. It's not about singing; it's all about viewing figures, making fun of someone else in public. Mockery sells. Unfortunately, malicious pleasure seems to be the best pleasure by many and has always been.

However, people's fear also relates to their immediate social environment, families, friends, and co-workers.
Strangely enough, we think less about how embarrassing a wrong gesture, a poor posture, or inappropriate glances could be in just the same environment; or clothes that don't fit, some extra 30 to 50 pounds on our hips, a bad hairstyle, being unshaved, scruffy fingernails, or crooked teeth.

The voice is particularly significant for a person. More than your outer appearance, it is your voice that reflects your personality.

This phenomenon is especially striking in the Oscar-winning movie "The King's Speech," and I would like to mention the end of the film to motivate everyone who still might hesitate to start singing:

Out of love for his people and his country, King George made great efforts to improve his voice to give speeches.
He did not become a great speaker, and his speaking was nothing special, neither in terms of rhetoric, voice power, nor a beautiful vocal color. But everyone in the audience immediately understood George's love for his people, his truthfulness, and his courage to take over responsibility.

Life is not always about perfection and high performance.

Life is actually about love.

Sing for love
- of music
- of life
- of yourself.

POSTFACE

Some final advice:
Begin with easy songs. And yes, even as an adult, you may begin with nursery rhymes if you have no better idea.

As a teacher for many years, a couple of evergreens became good songs to start with singing. I don't want to mention any titles because there are so many beautiful songs, and your taste might differ from mine. When you choose a piece, make sure that the range of the melody, from the lowest to the highest tone, is not so extreme – not reaching too low, neither too high. Fifty percent or more of all songs and hits have a range that exceeds a scale by one or two notes only. With a bit of practice, you will easily manage them!
It is also crucial that you choose the right key.
If the original song includes low or high tones that you cannot sing at the correct pitch - at least not yet at the moment - it simply doesn't make sense to sing the song - unless you can find a transposed version in another key. However, often, the song doesn't sound any good after transposing. So that doesn't pay.
Even for professional singers, sometimes, a song simply doesn't fit the voice. Then choose another piece; there are plenty of them. Seriously.
When you want to learn a song, listen to the music carefully – many times.
Many people start singing according to the motto "let's go," as soon as they like a song and memorized just the refrain. But that is not the complete song. Learn the entire melody. Listen carefully to find out how far the tones are apart. If you were wrong, listen again and give it another try. Don't keep singing past it.
Listen and learn.
The ear-voice connection is the key factor for musical sense – you can train that!

Don't cheat. Don't ever tell yourself: "Well, nobody will notice anyway." If you know that something is wrong, the audience will also notice.

Be honest with yourself and your audience.

If you are not fully committed to a song, then don't sing it.

These days, being authentic has become more critical than ever before.

For everyone who knows that Photoshop and VoiceTone can correct crinkles and wrong tones, honesty, passion, and love of music make a big difference.

Although performed with a perfect singing technique, many a voice remains unsuccessful simply because the singer lacks personality. The audience can feel it.

Never sing to please somebody.

Don't sing in a certain way or manner, just because you think it should be like that.

The only thing that matters is what feels good and what do you feel comfortable with.

If you are happy and honestly satisfied with your musical performance, you know that your voice sounds beautiful, and your performance is "carefully crafted." Then, you have the best preconditions to make other people happy and yourself too.

If you sing because it makes you happy, many happy moments will follow as of itself.

Singing enriches your life. You will be amazed at all the positive effects it brings along.

I wish you a lot of joy and happiness with singing.

"SINGING makes you HAPPY" is on my heart.

Therefore, I would like to ask all readers to think of those that might not have been so lucky in life.

Visit hospitals, older people's private homes, and caring homes, prisons, and orphanages and sing with the people there.
You will experience how much happiness you give to them - and yourself!
Believe me, it is just as moving as singing in front of 12,000 people in a big concert hall.

This way, you can even do good with what makes you happy.

DOWNLOAD TRACKS

All MP3 audio files are available for download on
https://www.christinbonin.com/singing-makes-you-happy

List of tracks:

Track 1   Exercise 1: Warming Up and Voice Placement Exercise

Track 2   Exercise 2: Activating your voice support

Track 3   Exercise 3: Building up energy

Track 4   Exercise 4: Increasing energy and managing air

Track 5   Exercise 5: Softly awakening your chest register

Track 6   Exercise 6: Developing vocal color

Track 7   Exercise 7: Changing sound

Track 8   Exercise 8: Sound variations

Track 9   Singing exercise *La-la-la*

Track 10   Singing exercise *Street of dreams*

Track 11   Singing exercise *Christmas under Palm Trees*

ENJOY YOUR TRAINING!

ACKNOWLEDGMENT

I gratefully acknowledge Gunter Hansen and Gerhard Schlegel for their amusing, funny illustrations. As on my Audio-CD "Single Well," they have captured the absolute essence of what I want to communicate! Thanks to Michel Bonin for taking care of the graphics, the cover design, and the layouts.

Special thanks to my students who keep telling me how singing makes them happy and how much I support them in achieving it.
Thanks to my audience, that keeps confirming that they can feel how passionate I am and how much they love it.

Thanks to the music for being there.

Christin Bonin

You want to continue and learn more?

CHRISTIN BONIN offers personal advice, individual lessons, work-shops, and masterclasses.

For further information, please write to:

chrbonin@icloud.com

Also available:

https://www.christinbonin.com/belt-voice-training

Check regularly for new publications on:

https://www.christinbonin.com/publications